Why do you celebrate Christmas?

WHAT WOULD BE THE BEST THING TO FIND IN A CRACKER?

What does a 'proper' Christmas need?

What are you most looking forward to this Christmas?

1

# NAZARETH

**What happened here over 2000 years ago that still makes a difference to our lives today?**

LEBANON

NAZARETH

JERUSALEM

BETHLEHEM

SYRIA

ISRAEL

EGYPT

(ROUGHLY HOW IT LOOKED BACK TH

*God* sent a MESSENGER to a young girl called **Mary**. The MESSENGER said,

> Mary, you're going to have God's baby. He will be the greatest rescuer in history. His name will mean "God saves".

**Mary** said, I'll do whatever God asks me to.

3

SHEPHERDS:
YOU MAY
SPEND YOUR
WHOLE LIFE
WONDERING,
'WHAT MIGHT
I HAVE
FOUND...?' GO
TO PAGE 21.

# QUEST

You're **Mary**, LISTENING TO
THE MESSENGER.

DO YOU SAY
**YES** OR **NO**

(GO TO PAGE 28 AND
LOOK FOR THE RED)

(GO TO PAGE 20 AND
LOOK FOR THE RED)

he MESSENGER also came to **JOSEPH** in a dream.

Stick by Mary!

*Draw Joseph's man-shed around him.*

5

The **government** made **EVERYONE** travel to where they were born in order to fill in **official forms.**

*Mary* and *JOSEPH* had to go about **80 miles** to **Bethlehem.**

It was a **TOUGH JOURNEY** for *Mary* and *JOSEPH*

**Circle the things that might help this Messy family on their tough journey.**

| 32 | 33 | 34 | 35 Joseph tells Mary off for singing too loudly |
|---|---|---|---|
| 31 Someone offers a bed for the night— no bedbugs! | 30 | 29 | 28 |
| 16 | 17 Mary gets very bored with the journey | 18 | 19 They see parts of the country they've never seen before |
| 15 | 14 | 13 | 12 |
| START at Nazareth | 1 | 2 | 3 Joseph rubs Mary's back when she gets tired |

8 SNAKES AND LADDERS

| | | |
|---|---|---|
| **37** | **38** The place they stay is so expensive! | **FINISH at Bethlehem** ⭐ |
| **26** | **25** | **24** |
| **21** | **22** | **23** |
| **10** | **9** The luggage is really heavy | **8** |
| **5** | **6** | **7** It's nice to be just the two of them, away from Nazareth |

# BETHLEHEM GAME

*Mary* and *JOSEPH* arrived in **Bethlehem**, but the town was full.

### CENSUS FORM

**You must get this form signed by everybody present in your house today.**

Name:

**Name:**

Name:

**Name:**

Name:

**Name:**

By order of the Emperor Augustus

# scavenger hunt

*Leave one person on your sofa. Everyone else, run round the house and see who can find...*

Something to do with welcome

SOMETHING NICE FOR SORE FEET

SOMETHING TO DO WITH A BABY

Something for Mary to rest on

Something to sign the census form with

# Where could they stay?

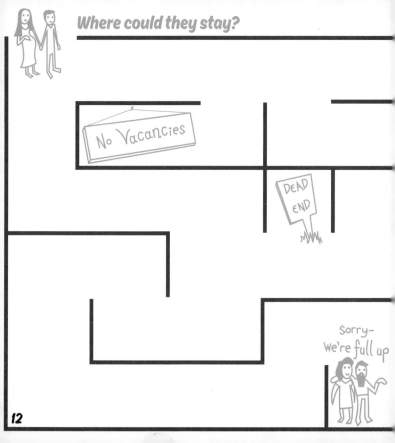

No Vacancies

DEAD END

Sorry—
We're full up

# JESUS' BIRTH

While **Mary** and **JOSEPH** were in **Bethlehem** their baby was born. They wrapped him in *strips of cloth* and put him in the only place there was space for him: an **ANIMALS' FEEDING BOX**.

*Draw Jesus in the hay...*

**Ask everyone in the room:**

| Where were you born? | What was the first bed you were put in? |
| --- | --- |
| | |
| | |
| | |
| | |
| | |
| | |
| | |
| | |
| | |

VISITORS:
JESUS IS KILLED BEFORE HE'S THREE YEARS OLD. GO TO PAGE 25.

# QUEST

You're **God**, THINKING HOW YOU WILL GIVE HUMAN BEINGS THE BEST POSSIBLE LIFE.

DO YOU

## STAY IN OR BECOME A BABY HEAVEN AND BE BORN ON EARTH

(GO TO PAGE 24 AND LOOK FOR THE PURPLE)

(GO TO PAGE 28 AND LOOK FOR THE PURPLE)

# Design a birthday cake under the candle.

# SHEPHERDS

Some shepherds were out on the hills outside **Bethlehem**, when a messenger appeared and said to them,

> Great news! *God's* rescuer has been born! You'll find him in **Bethlehem**, wrapped in *cloth* and lying in an ANIMALS' FEEDING BOX.

Suddenly the whole sky was filled with angels praising *God*.

*The word angel means 'God's messenger', but nobody knows what angels really look like. What do you think they look like?*

MARY: PACK ALL THE CHRISTMAS PRESENTS, FOOD AND DECORATIONS AWAY. THERE'S NOTHING TO CELEBRATE NOW. GO TO PAGE 5.

# QUEST

YOU'RE a shepherd.

DO YOU

## GO LOOKING FOR THIS BABY

OR

## STAY LOOKING AFTER YOUR SHEEP

(GO TO PAGE 28 AND LOOK FOR THE PINK)

(GO TO PAGE 4 AND LOOK FOR THE PINK)

So many babies in Bethlehem!
Can you find the right one?

Colour me in

21

Colou
me in

*So many sorts of chocolate! So many sorts of peop*
*are welcome to belong to Jesus' family! Colour in th*
*chocolates and make sure your favourite is there to*

ome time later, **some** visitors **from another country**
**rived in JERUSALEM and asked *KING HEROD*,**

Where is the new king? When we were
stargazing, we saw a special star appear for a
new king in this kingdom and we've come to
worship him.

**he holy books said a king would be born in**
**ethlehem. So *HEROD* sent the** visitors **there.**

*COME BACK AND TELL ME WHERE HE IS,*
*SO THAT I CAN WORSHIP HIM TOO.*

**he** visitors **set off to Bethlehem, found**
**esus and his family, worshipped him and gave**
**m presents of gold, frankincense and myrrh.**

23

GOD: WELL, IT'S NICE AND SAFE HERE AND NOTHING CAN GO WRONG. GO TO PAGE 17.

# QUEST

YOU'RE ONE OF THE visitors AND YOU'VE JUST SEEN **Jesus**.

DO YOU GO AND TELL *HEROD* WHERE HE IS?

## YES OR NO

(GO TO PAGE 16 AND LOOK FOR THE ORANGE)

(GO TO PAGE 28 AND LOOK FOR THE ORANGE)

What were the visitors' thoughts at seeing Jesus, the unexpected king?

*KING HEROD* was furious that the visitors hadn't told him where **Jesus** was. He wanted to kill **Jesus**.

*JOSEPH* had a dream warning him of the danger and escaped with **Mary** and **Jesus** to Egypt. But *HEROD'S* soldiers killed all the small boys who were in **Bethlehem**.

*Colour in these homes, then colour them again in a dark colour.*

Colour me in

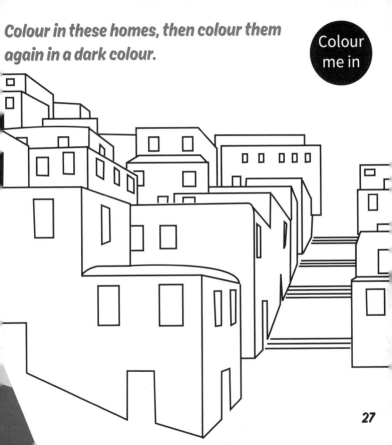

# QUEST
# Answers

MARY: THE ADVENTURE CAN KEEP GOING! GO TO PAGE 5.

GOD: YOU'VE DEFINITELY PICKED THE RISKIEST OPTION. GO TO PAGE 1

SHEPHERDS: WELL DONE! NOW PEOPLE WILL KNOW THAT JESUS THINKS MESSY PEOPLE ARE IMPORTANT. GO TO PAGE 21.

VISITORS: THERE'S A CHANCE FOR JESUS TO ESCAPE. GO TO PAGE 25.

THE PEOPLE IN THE STORY HAD TO CHOOSE THE RIGHT THING EACH TIME SO THAT *God's* PLAN COULD HAPPEN.

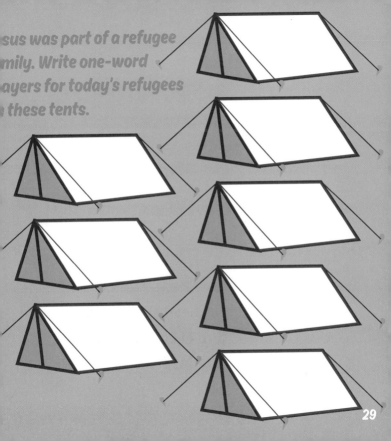

Jesus was part of a refugee family. Write one-word prayers for today's refugees in these tents.

29

When it was safe, **Mary, JOSEPH** and **Jesus** went back from Egypt to **NAZARETH.** **Jesus** grew older and wiser and everybody loved him... especially *God*.

Christmas is the time of year when we remind each other about when **Jesus** was born. There are many different ways to celebrate this happy news. We make sure nobody gets left out, because *God* sent **Jesus** to make sure everybody has the chance to be part of his family.

*This Christmas, how would you like to celebrate Jesus being born? Draw a picture of how you will celebrate Christmas in your home.*

**The Bible Reading Fellowship**
15 The Chambers, Vineyard
Abingdon OX14 3FE
**brf.org.uk**

Messy Church is part of The Bible Reading Fellowship, a Registered Charity (233280)

ISBN 978 0 85746 521 4
First published 2016
Reprinted 2016
10 9 8 7 6 5 4 3 2 1

Illustrations by Rebecca J Hall

A catalogue record for this book is available from the British Library

Printed in the UK by Rainbow Print (Wales) Ltd